Events

News for every

CW00860499

**Mary Pickford, one of the most popular
Hollywood stars of 1921.**

By Hugh Morrison

MONTPELIER PUBLISHING

Front cover: (clockwise from left): Poster for *The Sheik* starring Rudolf Valentino. Charlie Chaplin and Jackie Coogan star in *The Kid*. HRH Prince Edward, Prince of Wales. Contestants in the first Miss America pageant.

Back cover (clockwise from top): Rudolph Valentino in *The Four Horsemen of the Apocalypse*. The British Olympic running champion Mary Lines. The first British Legion Poppy. Outgoing US President Woodrow Wilson *(left)* with new incumbent Warren G Harding. The baseball star Babe Ruth. The body of the Unknown Soldier arrives at Washington Navy Yard.

Image credits: Heather Annej, Stephen Simpson, Paramount Pictures, Allan Warren, Agence Rol, Acme, Tony Hisgett, Walter Stoneman, New York Sunday News, Yesterday's Antique Motorcycles, The National Library of Ireland, National Photo Company Collection, Agence de Presse Meurise, Panyd, Boston Public Library, Theodor Andersen/Wilhelm Klem, Jozef Trylinski, Paul Thomson, EB Thompson, JLPC, Alduin 2000.

This edition © Montpelier Publishing 2020. All rights reserved.

ISBN: 9798697342268

January
1921

Saturday 1: Car tax discs are introduced in the United Kingdom.

The publishing firm Jonathan Cape is founded in Bloomsbury, London.

Sunday 2: The first religious radio broadcast is made on American radio, on KDKA in Pittsburgh.

Monday 3: The German submarine *UB-88*, seized by the US Navy in 1918, is sunk during target practice off the Californian coast.

A 1921 British car tax disc.

The first radio weather forecast is broadcast, on Station 9XM (now WHA) in Madison, Wisconsin.

Tuesday 4: US President Warren G Harding is inaugurated. It is the first inauguration broadcast on the radio.

Wednesday 5: 48 US Navy ships begin the largest military exercise in the nation's history.

January 1921

President Warren G Harding *(centre)* arrives for his inauguration in Washington, DC, on 4 January. On the left is the outgoing President, Woodrow Wilson.

Thursday 6: The British schooner *Marion* disappears off the Cornish coast; no trace of her or her crew is ever found.

Friday 7: Figures released on this day show that Britain's Royal Navy has double the strength of the US Navy.

Saturday 8: The estate of Chequers in Buckinghamshire near London becomes the official country residence of Britain's Prime Ministers in perpetuity.

Sunday 9: Daniel O'Callaghan, Mayor of Cork, is greeted by large crowds of Irish nationalists when he arrives in New York City.

Investment banker John B Millholland of Spokane, Washington, is found dead from suicide after being caught embezzling over $350,000 from clients.

Monday 10: The thrifty US President Elect Warren Harding announces that there will be minimal public celebrations of his inauguration.

Tuesday 11: Mrs Taylor Bumpstead becomes the first woman to serve on a British jury.

Wednesday 12: The British politician Winston Churchill is appointed Colonial Secretary.

Thursday 13: Two policemen of the Royal Irish Constabulary are shot dead by the IRA in Limerick; another two officers are killed in an ambush in Cratloe, near Dublin.

Friday 14: The US senate passes a law restricting the size of the army to 150,000 men.

Saturday 15: Japan's Mitsubishi Electric Corporation is formed.

Sunday 16: North Dublin is cordoned off by police and troops for systematic house to house searches following fierce fighting between British forces and Irish nationalists.

Monday 17: The first transcontinental radio message is sent across the USA, from Hartford, Connecticut, to Los Angeles, California, via a series of midwestern relay stations.

Chequers becomes the official country residence of the British Prime Minister on 8 January.

January 1921

Agatha Christie's first book is published on 21 January.

Tuesday 18: A major fire sweeps through the town of Worcester, Massachusetts, causing US$3m worth of damage.

Wednesday 19: The mystery writer Patricia Highsmith (*The Talented Mr Ripley*) is born in Fort Worth, Texas (died 1995).

Thursday 20: The Royal Navy submarine HMS *K5* sinks in the English Channel with the loss of all hands.

Friday 21: Agatha Christie's first detective novel, *The Mysterious Affair At Styles*, featuring Hercule Poirot, is first published.

Saturday 22: The multi-millionaire industrialist Alfred du Pont of the DuPont chemical empire marries Jessie Ball in Los Angeles, California.

Sunday 23: Talks begin between the US and Japanese governments on naturalization and land ownership rights for the large numbers of Japanese immigrants arriving in the USA.

Monday 24: The Allied Supreme Council begins talks in Paris on the disarmament of Germany.

Tuesday 25: An agreement on the rights of Japanese immigrants in the USA is reached.

Right: The Fatty Arbuckle comedy film *Brewster's Millions* is released on 28 January.

Wednesday 26: 17 people are killed in a train crash in Abermule, Montgomeryshire, Wales. The fatalities include the chairman of the railway company, Lord Herbert Vane-Tempest.

Thursday 27: During disarmament talks in Paris, the French government demands further occupation of Germany if reparations are not paid.

Friday 28: The silent comedy film *Brewster's Millions* starring Fatty Arbuckle is released.

Saturday 29: A cut of one billion dollars in US government expenditure is announced as part of President Warren Harding's economy drive.

Sunday 30: The Allied war reparations committee issues a demand of 132 billion marks (c.US$32 billion) from Germany.

Monday 31: The US Navy announces 43,000 job losses as part of the government economy drive.

Members of the Allied Supreme Council begin talks on 24 January. British Prime Minister David Lloyd George is second from left.

February 1921

Tuesday 1: The US government approves the repatriation of the body of an unidentified war casualty in France to be interred as the Unknown Warrior in the Arlington National Cemetery.

Wednesday 2: The German government announces it cannot pay the US$32 billion war reparations demanded by the Allies.

Thursday 3: 'Medicinal' alcohol from US pharmacists is restricted, due to suspicions that it is being sold for non-medical uses.

Friday 4: The US army stages a mock air-raid on Manhattan with 15 planes using smoke bombs and blank rounds as part of a recruitment drive.

Saturday 5: The serial killer Louise Peete is convicted of murder by a jury in Los Angeles; she is eventually executed in 1947.

Chaplin and Coogan star in *The Kid*.

February 1921

Russian Bolshevik troops arrive in the Georgian capital Tblisi on 25 February.

Sunday 6: The silent comedy drama film *The Kid* starring Charlie Chaplin and Jackie Coogan is released.

Monday 7: The silent drama film *The Skin Game* starring Edmund Glenn and Mary Clare, based on the play by John Galsworthy, is released.

Tuesday 8: The Hollywood star and 'sweater girl' Lana Turner is born in Wallace, Idaho (died 1995).

Wednesday 9: HM King George V and Queen Mary visit the International Advertising Exhibition at White City, London.

Thursday 10: 32 people are killed when a tornado hits the town of Oconee, Georgia.

Friday 11: The Japanese steamship *Fukuyo Maru* is impounded at Galveston, Texas, after 11 stowaways are found on board as part of an alleged people-smuggling operation.

Saturday 12: Russian Bolshevik forces invade the Democratic Republic of Georgia.

February 1921

Rezā Khan seizes power in Iran on 21 February.

The Allied Conference of London, on the future of the Ottoman Empire, defeated in the First World War, begins.

Sunday 13: Dr William Duane, professor of biophysics at the University of Harvard, announces a new method of using x-rays to treat cancer.

Monday 14: Police in Paris claim to have foiled a communist plot to overthrow the governments of France, Spain and Italy on 1 May.

Tuesday 15: HM King George V attends the State Opening of Parliament and warns against disunity in Ireland in his speech.

Wednesday 16: The National Women's Party convention in Washington DC calls for 'absolute equality' and women's right to vote.

Thursday 17: Thousands of messages of support are received by the opera singer Enrico Caruso, seriously ill following a heart attack. He dies on 2 August.

Friday 18: Britain's Colonial Secretary recommends self-government for the protectorate of Egypt.

Saturday 19: Bolshevik troops overrun Georgia as the country's government flees from the capital Tblisi.

Actress Lana Turner is born on 8 February.

February 1921

Boys sledging in New York City after heavy snowfall on 20 February.

Sunday 20: 11 inches of snow fall on New York City as severe storms batter the north-eastern USA.

Monday 21: Rezā Khan seizes power in a coup d'état in Iran.

Tuesday 22: Sergeant Encil Chambers of the US Army sets the world parachute jump height record at 22,000 feet (6705m) when he leaps from an airship near Fort Sill, Oklahoma.

Wednesday 23: US Airmail pilots deliver post from San Francisco to New York City in a record 33 hours and 20 minutes.

Thursday 24: Lt William D Coney, US Army Air Service, becomes the first pilot to cross the continental USA in under 24 hours.

Friday 25: The Red Army enters the Georgian capital of Tblisi and installs a Soviet government.

Saturday 26: The actress and singer Betty Hutton is born in Battle Creek, Michigan (died 2007).

Sunday 27: 30 people are killed when two express trains collide near Porter, Indiana.

Monday 28: The Kronstadt Rebellion: Russian sailors mutiny against Soviet leaders in the last major resistance to the communist takeover of Russia.

March 1921

Tuesday 1: The Australian cricket team becomes the first to achieve an Ashes series whitewash (winning every match) when it defeats England 5-0. The feat is not repeated for 86 years.

Wednesday 2: The prominent US politician and Speaker of the House of Representatives Champ Clark dies aged 70.

Thursday 3: On his last day in office, US President Wilson abolishes nearly all emergency laws brought in during the First World War.

Friday 4: Warren G Harding is sworn in as the 29th President of the United States.

Saturday 5: Brigadier General Hanway Robert Cumming DSO becomes the highest ranking British officer to be killed in the Irish uprising.

Sunday 6: The highest grossing film of 1921, *The Four Horsemen of the Apocalypse*, starring Rudolph Valentino, is released.

Rudolf Valentino stars in *The Four Horsemen of the Apocalypse*.

Monday 7: Large fires spread across the Russian city of Petrograd as counter-revolutionaries rise up against the Bolshevik government.

Tuesday 8: The Prime Minister of Spain, Eduardo Dato, is assassinated by Catalan nationalists.

Allied forces occupy the German cities of Dusseldorf, Ruhrort and Duisburg.

Wednesday 9: Australia assumes control of the former German colony of New Guinea.

Edith Cowan OBE becomes Australia's first woman MP on 12 March.

Thursday 10: German troops fire on a French patrol in Upper Silesia as the Allied occupation of the Rhineland continues.

Friday 11: HM Queen Mary becomes the first woman to be awarded an honorary degree by Oxford University.

Saturday 12: Edith Cowan becomes the first woman Member of Parliament in Australia.

Sunday 13: The czarist Russian White Army captures Mongolia from China.

Monday 14: Six Irish nationalists are executed in Mountjoy Prison, Dublin, for their part in attacks on Crown forces in Ireland.

Tuesday 15: Five people die when fire breaks out in a Pullman train carriage near Walsenburg, Colorado.

Left: Spain's Prime Minister, Eduardo Dato, is assassinated on 8 March.

March 1921

Wednesday 16: Critical food shortages are reported in Moscow as counter-revolutionaries continue their uprising against the Soviets.

Thursday 17: Dr Marie Stopes opens the first family planning clinic in London.

Friday 18: The Peace of Riga ends the Polish-Soviet War.

Saturday 19: The comedian Tommy Cooper is born in Caerphilly, Wales (died 1984).

The comedian Tommy Cooper is born on 19 March.

British athlete Mary Lines wins five Gold Medals in the 1921 Womens' Olympiad.

Sunday 20: The province of Upper Silesia votes in a referendum to become part of Germany rather than Poland.

Monday 21: Nine British soldiers of the Royal Fusiliers are killed in an IRA ambush at Headford, County Kerry.

Tuesday 22: Large amounts of jewellery thought to belong to the late Czar of Russia are confiscated by Italian authorities from the Soviet embassy in Rome.

Wednesday 23: The British writer E W Hornung, creator of the 'gentleman thief' Raffles, dies aged 54.

Thursday 24: The first international women's sporting event, the Women's Olympiad, begins in Monte Carlo.

Friday 25 (Good Friday): A failed assassination attempt is made on the Italian Prime Minister, Giovanni Giolitti.

Saturday 26: Shaun Spadah, ridden by Fred Rees, wins the Grand National at odds of 100/9. It is the only horse out of 35 to complete the race without falling.

Sunday 27 (Easter Sunday): Communists clash with police in Berlin and Hamburg as industrial unrest spreads across Germany.

The actor Sir Dirk Bogarde is born on 28 March.

Monday 28: The actor Sir Dirk Bogarde is born in Birmingham, England (died 1999).

Tuesday 29: The pioneering US conservationist John Burroughs dies aged 83.

Wednesday 30: Cambridge wins the 1921 Oxford v Cambridge Boat Race on the River Thames in London.

Thursday 31: Wartime government control of British coal mines is lifted, and immediately followed by wage reductions.

April
1921

Friday 1: The first British civilian airship, R36, makes its maiden flight.

Saturday 2: HM King Charles IV of Hungary, deposed in 1918, makes an unsuccessful attempt to regain his throne. He is later arrested by occupying British forces and sent into exile.

His Majesty the Blessed Charles IV, King of Hungary, fails to regain the throne on 2 April.

Sunday 3: 12,000 people are made homeless following a major fire in Manila in the Phillippines.

Monday 4: The British government takes over control of all coal mining and production and puts troops on standby in response to a nationwide miners' strike.

Tuesday 5: A Mercury aeroplane sets the record for the fastest passenger flight between Los Angeles and San Diego, California, at 1 hour 30 minutes.

Wednesday 6: Britain's coal mining unions agree to talks with mine owners to settle the crippling national mining strike.

Thursday 7: Six people are killed and 35 injured in a train crash near New River, Tennessee.

Friday 8: Britain puts all military reservists on standby as talks between striking coal miners and pit owners break down.

Saturday 9: A general strike in Britain becomes less likely as coal mining unions resume talks with mine authorities.

Sunday 10: The singer Sheb Wooley, best known for his 1958 hit *Purple People Eater*, is born in Erick, Oklahoma.

Monday 11: The British protectorate of the Emirate of Transjordan is created, under Emir Abdullah the First.

A Bolshevik plot to subvert the British Army is uncovered by London police.

Emir Abdullah I with Sir Herbert Samuel, High Commissioner, and Winston Churchill, Colonial Secretary, at the creation of the British Protectorate of Transjordan.

April 1921

Programme for the 1921 FA Cup Final at Wembley Stadium, London.

Tuesday 12: The new US President, Warren Harding, urges Congress to make peace with Germany, with whom the USA has technically still been at war since the Armistice of 1918.

Wednesday 13: Rioting breaks out in thirteen cities across Britain as the government announces that troops will be used to protect workers breaking the coal miners' strike.

Thursday 14: US Prohibition authorities release figures showing that bootleggers made nearly one billion dollars from the sale of illegal alcohol in 1920.

Friday 15: 'Black Friday': British trade unions decide not to call for a general strike over wage reductions for coal miners.

Sir Peter Ustinov is born on 16 April.

Saturday 16: The writer, actor and raconteur Sir Peter Ustinov is born in London (died 2004).

Sunday 17: 120 people are killed in severe storms in the Mississippi Valley, while Iowa is brought to a standstill as five inches of snow fall in one day.

Monday 18: A meeting of the Allied Supreme Council is scheduled after it is announced that Germany has defaulted on its war debt repayments.

Tuesday 19: The Allied Supreme Councils serves a three day ultimatum to Germany to resume its war reparations payments.

Wednesday 20: The Barcelona Convention is ratified, allowing mariners freedom to use most international waterways.

Thursday 21: 13 people are killed in violent clashes between fascists and communists in Italy.

Friday 22: The US government agrees to act as an independent mediator in war reparations discussions between Germany and the western Allies.

Saturday 23: Tottenham Hotspur beat Wolverhampton Wanderers 1-0 in England's Football Association (FA) Cup Final.

The US athlete Charles Paddock sets a world record for the 100m sprint at 10.2 seconds.

Sunday 24: One police officer is killed and two injured in an IRA attack on a police station in Kilrush, County Clare; in another IRA attack two hundred men loot and set fire to a train in County Monaghan.

Monday 25: The British government announces that it will support France in military occupation of Germany if war reparations demands are not met.

Tuesday 26: Federal agents in St Paul, Minnesota, investigate an alleged plot by the Communist Party of America to start a revolution on May Day.

The record-breaking US sprinter Charles Paddock.

April 1921

Marshal Joffre is put in charge of the Allied occupation force for Germany on 29 April.

Wednesday 27: The Allied reparations commission announces that Germany must pay US$33 billion in war reparations.

Thursday 28: Britain joins France in formally rejecting Germany's counter-offer to repay reduced war reparations over a period of 40 years.

Thousands of acres of crops are ruined following severe flooding in the Black River area of Missouri.

Friday 29: Marshal Joffre, head of French forces in the Great War, is appointed head of an Allied invasion force should Germany refuse to make war reparations.

Saturday 30: The French army is mobilised, with forces moved towards the German border; Great Britain gives Germany 12 days to agree to war reparations before she also mobilises her troops.

May
1921

Sunday 1: Serious rioting breaks out between Jews and Arabs in Jaffa, British Mandatory Palestine (now Israel).

Monday 2: Poles in Silesia rise up against their new German government following the plebiscite of 20 March.

Tuesday 3: The partition of Ireland takes place into the British province of Northern Ireland and the semi-autonomous state of Southern Ireland.

The boxer Sugar Ray Robinson is born in Ailey, Georgia (died 1989).

Sugar Ray Robinson is born on 3 May.

Wednesday 4: Martial law is imposed by occupying Allied troops in Upper Silesia following clashes between Poles and Germans.

Thursday 5: Only 13 paying spectators attend an English Football League match between Leicester City and Stockport County; it is the lowest attendance ever for a League game.

Friday 6: Germany officially recognises the Soviet regime in Russia.

May 1921

Saturday 7: Crown Prince Hirohito of Japan makes a state visit to the United Kingdom.

'Behave Yourself' ridden by Charles Thompson wins the Kentucky Derby.

Japan's Prince Hirohito visits Oxford, England.

Sunday 8: French troops occupy Muelheim in Germany's Ruhr district following Germany's failure to make war reparations payments.

Monday 9: Luigi Pirandello's controversial play *Six Characters in Search of an Author* is first shown in Rome.

Tuesday 10: A 700-mile stretch of Mexico's coastline is ravaged by devastating forest fires.

The serial killer Lyda Trueblood is arrested on 12 May.

Wednesday 11: Germany accepts in full the Allied war reparation demands of US$33 billion and surrenders all military capability.

Thursday 12: The serial killer Lyda 'Bluebeard' Trueblood, 27, is arrested in Honolulu on suspicion of killing four former husbands, her daughter and brother-in-law with arsenic. She is found guilty and sentenced to life imprisonment six weeks later.

Friday 13: A three day geomagnetic storm caused by sunspots begins. Telegraph signals in the USA are disrupted and a fire breaks out in New York's Grand Central station due to damaged electrical equipment.

Saturday 14: Troops are called in to end gun battles between striking miners and strike-breakers in Williamson, West Virginia.

Sunday 15: The British Legion, (later the Royal British Legion), the charity for British ex-servicemen, is formed under the patronage of Earl Haig.

Monday 16: 20 people are killed as violence worsens between nationalists and Crown forces across Ireland.

Tuesday 17: A gun battle breaks out between the IRA and police at a football match in Cork, Ireland.

Wednesday 18: Prime Minister David Lloyd George states that British forces will be sent to Germany's Upper Silesia region if insurgency by Polish nationalists occurs.

Thursday 19: The US government introduces the Emergency Quota Act, severely restricting European immigration.

British troops search for IRA gunmen on a railway line in County Kerry.

May 1921

Michael Llewelyn Davies, the foster son of the writer JM Barrie and the inspiration for the character Peter Pan, is drowned in a swimming accident aged 20.

Friday 20: French army reservists called up to occupy Germany mutiny at Dijon; the uprising is suppressed by regular troops.

Saturday 21: The funeral of Edward Douglass White, former US Chief Justice who died on 19 May, takes place in Washington and is marked by a seventeen gun salute from the Pacific Fleet.

Pope Benedict XV.

Sunday 22: Pope Benedict XV appeals for peace in Ireland, asking that a miniature 'League of Nations' be set up in the country to promote unity.

Monday 23: The Leipzig War Crimes Trials begin of German war criminals.

The jazz trumpeter and broadcaster Humphrey Littleton is born in Eton, Berkshire (died 2008).

Tuesday 24: Ulster Unionists win 40 out of 52 seats in the first Northern Ireland general election.

Wednesday 25: The IRA seizes and burns down the Dublin Custom House, the centre of local government for Southern Ireland; British troops capture 80 IRA activists during the action.

Thursday 26: A general strike begins in Norway.

Friday 27: The Colorado Mothers' Congress denounces 'ill behaved children who attend the movies and throw chewing gum from the balcony', calling for a return to the 'old-fashioned mother whose children knew how to behave'.

The Dublin Custom House in flames during the IRA attack of 25 May.

Saturday 28: The American Legion holds the first 'Poppy Day' to raise funds for war wounded. Britain and Commonwealth countries follow suit in November.

Sunday 29: US President Harding pays tribute to America's war dead at Arlington National Cemetery.

Monday 30: Edith Wharton becomes the first woman to win the Pulitzer Prize for Fiction, for her novel *The Age of Innocence*.

Tuesday 31: A two-day race riot begins in Tulsa, Oklahoma.

June
1921

Wednesday 1: The Epsom Derby is won by Humorist; it is the first Derby to broadcast live on the radio.

The composer and bandleader Nelson Riddle is born in Oradell, New Jersey (died 1985).

Thursday 2: Planning permission for what eventually becomes the Hoover Dam is applied for by the Southern California Edison Company.

Friday 3: Christians are massacred by Muslims in Armenia; the US Navy sends a destroyer to protect US citizens in the region.

London's Southwark Bridge, begun in 1913, opens on 6 June.

James Craig, first Prime Minister of Northern Ireland.

Saturday 4: Approximately 3000 people are thought drowned in catastrophic flooding in Pueblo, Colorado.

Sunday 5: Two American soldiers of the army of occupation are killed during rioting at Andrach, Germany.

Monday 6: HM King George V opens London's Southwark Bridge.

Tuesday 7: James Craig is elected as the first Prime Minister of Northern Ireland.

Wednesday 8: The US army carries out the first experimental aeroplane cabin pressurisation in a de Havilland DH4.

Thursday 9: The city of Pueblo, Colorado, is placed under martial law following its devastation by flooding.

Friday 10: Unemployment in the United Kingdom reaches 2.2 million.

HRH Prince Philip, husband of HM Queen Elizabeth II, is born in Corfu, Greece.

DH Lawrence's novel *Women in Love* is first published.

Saturday 11: Turkish leader Mustapha Kemal Ataturk signs a treaty with Soviet Russia for aid in fighting Greece.

Sunday 12: Sunday postal deliveries are abolished in the UK.

HRH Prince Philip is born on 10 June.

June 1921

Monday 13: The US Army and Navy sink three captured German ships in Chesapeake Bay in experiments to test the effectiveness of fighter aircraft against ships.

The 1921 USA polo team.

Tuesday 14: The orchestral piece *The Lark Ascending* by Vaughan Williams is performed for the first time by the British Symphony Orchestra conducted by Sir Adrian Boult at Queen's Hall, London.

Wednesday 15: Prohibition ends in British Columbia, Canada.

Thursday 16: Britain's Howard R Davies wins the Isle of Man Senior TT race with an average speed of 54.49mph on an AJS 349cc motorcycle.

Friday 17: London's railways are brought to a standstill as IRA terrorists set fire to signal boxes across the capital; in the worst incident in Bromley, Kent, six arsonists are arrested after shooting a police constable.

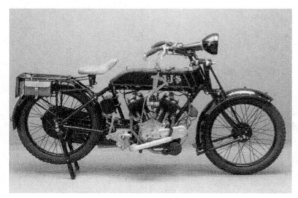

An AJS 349cc motorcycle of the type ridden by the 1921 TT Races winner Howard R Davies.

Sir Hamar Greenwood, Chief Secretary for Ireland, arrives in ceremonial dress for the State Opening of the Parliament of Northern Ireland on 22 July.

Saturday 18: The visiting US polo team defeat the British side 11 to 4 in the International Polo Cup at Hurlingham, England, attended by HM King George V.

Sunday 19: The census of the United Kingdom is taken.

The actor Louis Jourdan is born in Marseilles, France (died 2015).

Monday 20: US government officials announce that three American cargo ships have been seized on the high seas by the Soviets, and their contents confiscated.

Tuesday 21: The actress Jane Russell is born in Bemidji, Minnesota (died 2011).

The hit song *Second Hand Rose* sung by Fanny Brice is first performed.

June 1921

Britain's *R38* airship makes its maiden flight from Cardington, Bedfordshire, on 24 July.

Wednesday 22: HM King George V opens the newly formed Parliament of Northern Ireland.

Thursday 23: Following unrest in Ireland, the British parliament debates the introduction of compulsory passport checks for all Irish visitors to mainland Britain.

Friday 24: The *R38*, the world's largest airship, makes its maiden flight from Bedfordshire, England.

Saturday 25: Jock Hutchison wins the 1921 British Open golf tournament at St Andrews, Scotland.

Sunday 26: The Anglo-French secret agent, Violette Szabo GC, whose heroic wartime service inspires the film *Carve Her Name With Pride*, is born in Paris, France (died 1945).

Monday 27: The signing of the last Numbered Treaties takes place, concluding land-use negotiations between the British Empire and the indigenous peoples of Canada.

Tuesday 28: The newly created nation of Yugoslavia passes its first Constitution.

Wednesday 29: Lady Randolph Churchill, the American mother of the future British Prime Minister Sir Winston Churchill, dies aged 67.

Thursday 30: Sweden abolishes the death penalty.

July
1921

Friday 1: The Communist Party of China is founded.

Saturday 2: The USA formally ends its state of war with Germany, Austria and Hungary.

The Wimbledon Tennis Championships are won by Bill Tilden (USA) and Suzanne Lenglen (France).

Jack Dempsey beats Georges Carpentier in the first boxing match to be broadcast on radio.

Wimbledon tennis champion Suzanne Lenglen.

Sunday 3: The Order of the Falcon, Iceland's only order of chivalry, is founded by King Christian X of Denmark and Iceland.

Monday 4: Over 10,000 Americans drive into British Columbia to celebrate the Fourth of July in prohibition-free Canada.

July 1921

Gabriel Poulain *(right)* with his 'Aviette' flying bicycle.

Tuesday 5: The Great War Veterans' Association of Canada adopts the poppy as its symbol.

Wednesday 6: Russian Bolshevik troops clash with Japanese forces at Novomichiankievsk.

Nancy Reagan, First Lady of the United States, is born in New York City (died 2016).

Thursday 7: A severe heatwave hits the US eastern states, with shops and factories closed due to unbearable temperatures.

Nancy Reagan is born on 6 July.

Friday 8: The comedian Charlie Chaplin is sued by lawyers in Salt Lake City, Utah, who claim he owes them $25,000 in legal fees connected with his divorce from actress Mildred Harris.

Saturday 9: French cyclist Gabriel Poulain wins a prize of 10,000 francs when he becomes the first person to pilot a pedal-powered aeroplane, making a brief flight of 35 feet at an altitude of three feet.

Sunday 10: 16 people are killed in clashes between Protestants and Catholics in Belfast, Northern Ireland.

Monday 11: British and IRA forces agree to a ceasefire, ending the Irish War of Independence.

Tuesday 12: Harry Hawker, founder of Hawker Aircraft, is killed in a plane crash near Hendon Aerodrome. HM King George V's message of condolence reads 'The nation has lost one of its most distinguished airmen'.

Aviation pioneer Harry Hawker is killed on 12 July.

Wednesday 13: The Anglo-Japanese Alliance, dating from 1902, is lapsed as the British government moves towards closer alliance with the USA.

Thursday 14: In a widely publicised case, two Italian anarchists, Nicola Sacco and Bartolomeo Vanzetti are found guilty of first degree murder,for the killing of two people during an armed robbery in 1920.

Friday 15: Greek forces occupy the city of Afium Karahissar in western Turkey.

Saturday 16: Pilot JH James wins the sixth Aerial Derby in London, in a Gloster Mars with an average speed of 163.34mph.

Sunday 17: The short-lived Republic of Mirdita between Albania and Serbia is proclaimed.

Monday 18: The first BCG vaccination against tuberculosis is administered.

Tuesday 19: Rev Philip Irwin, minister of St Anne's Episcopal

July 1921

Augusto Ferrer-Dalmau's painting of the Battle of Annual, *The Charge of the Spanish 14th Cavalry*.

church, Orlando, Florida, is kidnapped and beaten by masked men after preaching about racial equality to his largely black congregation.

Wednesday 20: At least seven oil wells are reported to be on fire as a major conflagration sweeps the oil district of Amatlan, Mexico.

Thursday 21: Spanish colonial troops are defeated by Berbers at the Battle of Annual in Morocco.

Friday 22: The British golfer Jim Barnes wins the 1921 US Open golf tournament at Chevy Chase, Maryland.

Saturday 23: The Communist Party of China holds its first national congress in Shanghai, with fifty members.

Sunday 24: Belgium's Léon Scieur wins the Tour de France bicycle race.

Monday 25: US boxer Pete Herman defeats Joe Lynch in the World Bantamweight title match in Ebbet's Field, New York.

Tuesday 26: An imposter named Stanley Clifford Weyman, posing as a US State Department official, engineers a meeting with President Warren G Harding and tricks $10,000 out of a visiting dignitary, Princess Fatima of Afghanistan.

Wednesday 27: Researchers at the University of Toronto led by Frederick Banting announce the discovery of Insulin.

Thursday 28: The Church of Scotland Act 1921 confirms the Church of Scotland as the 'national church' but independent of state control.

Britain's Jim Barnes, winner of the 1921 US Open golf tournament on 22 July.

Friday 29: Adolf Hitler becomes leader of the Nazi party.

Saturday 30: French colonial police close down the first national congress of the Chinese Communist Party in Shanghai.

Sunday 31: 18 people are killed when fascist demonstrators clash with police in Sarzana, Italy.

August
1921

Monday 1: The first congress of the South African Communist Party ends.

Tuesday 2: The opera singer Enrico Caruso dies aged 48.

Wednesday 3: The first crop duster plane is flown, in Dayton, Ohio.

The opera singer Enrico Caruso dies on 2 August.

Thursday 4: The US Navy submarine *S-12* is launched at Portsmouth, New Hampshire.

Friday 5: The first radio broadcast of a baseball game is made from station Westinghouse KDKA in Pittsburgh.

Saturday 6: The Allied Supreme Council recommends the German district of Upper Silesia be awarded to Poland.

Sunday 7: 48 people are killed when the passenger ship SS *Alaska* sinks off the coast of northern California.

The Macchi M7 hydroplane.

Monday 8: Giovanni De Briganti wins the 1921 Schneider Trophy air race at Venice, Italy, in a Macchi M7 with an average speed of 189.7 km/h (117.9 mph).

Tuesday 9: The US senate approves the Willis-Campbell Act allowing for doctors to prescribe spirits and wine (but not beer) for medical purposes, despite prohibition.

Wednesday 10: The SS *Moerdijk* of the Holland-American steam line sets a world speed record, completing a journey from London to Los Angeles in 24 days and 12 hours.

Thursday 11: A heatwave sweeps central Europe, with temperatures peaking at 39C (102F) in Breslau, Poland.

Friday 12: A US destroyer is despatched to watch the British schooner *Arethusa*, said to be selling liquor off the Massachusetts coast.

Saturday 13: Stormont Castle is established as the official residence of the Prime Minister of Northern Ireland.

Stormont Castle becomes the official residence of the Prime Minister of Northern Ireland on 13 August.

August 1921

Irish Catholics hold a prayer vigil outside the Anglo-Irish peace talks in Whitehall, London.

Sunday 14: An earthquake measuring 6.1 hits Massawa in Eritrea.

Monday 15: Peace talks between Britain and the provisional government of southern Ireland begin in London.

Tuesday 16: The British government announces a stark choice for Irish nationalists in peace talks: accept Dominion status (similar to Canada and Australia) or have all home rule removed.

Wednesday 17: Irish leader Eamonn de Valera rejects Britain's peace offer and calls upon nationalists to defend the Irish Republic.

Thursday 18: The US government announces an aid package for Russia following its recent famine.

Secret peace talks take place on 22 August between Irish politician Eamon de Valera *(left)* and IRA leader Michael Collins.

Friday 19: Britain's railway companies are combined into the 'Big Four' of LMS, LNER, GWR and SR.

Saturday 20: Tennis player Molla Mallory wins the 1921 US National Championships.

Sunday 21: The notorious serial killer Carl Grossmann, thought to have killed up to 100 women, is arrested in Berlin, Germany.

Monday 22: Secret peace talks take place in Dublin between nationalist leader Eamonn de Valera and IRA leader Michael Collins.

Tuesday 23: King Faisal I of Iraq is crowned in Baghdad.

Wednesday 24: 44 people are killed when the British airship ZR-2 explodes near Kingston-upon-Hull.

Thursday 25: US politician Franklin Roosevelt contracts polio and is permanently crippled by the illness.

Left: **King Faisal I of Iraq.**

August 1921

The US-German Peace Treaty goes into effect, ending the state of war between the two nations.

Friday 26: Martial law is declared in Germany following the assassination of the finance minister, Matthias Erzberger.

Saturday 27: British Prime Minister David Lloyd George announces 'we cannot countenance separation' between Britain and Ireland.

Sunday 28: The silent film *The Three Musketeers* starring Douglas Fairbanks is released.

Douglas Fairbanks stars in *The Three Musketeers*, released on 28 August.

Monday 29: Loewe's State Theatre opens in New York City with a gala night attended by stars including Lionel Barrymore, Mary Pickford and Douglas Fairbanks.

Tuesday 30: Five people are killed in sectarian rioting in Belfast, Northern Ireland.

Martial law is declared in West Virginia following clashes between police and striking coal miners.

Wednesday 31: The prefix 'Royal' is awarded to the Australian Air Force by HM King George V.

Thursday 1: Nine borough councillors in Poplar, London, are arrested for organising a rate-payers' strike in protest over taxes.

September 1921

Friday 2: Associated Producers, a major motion picture company under Mack Sennett, is formed in the USA.

Saturday 3: The Dutch government orders all mail communications between Germany and the exiled Kaiser Wilhelm to be cut in order to stem a rise in German nationalism.

Sunday 4: 400 coal miners in West Virginia capitulate to regular US Army troops, ending the recent violent strike action.

Monday 5: The USA wins the 1921 International Lawn Tennis Challenge (later renamed the Davis Cup) at West Side Tennis Club, New York City.

The film comedian Roscoe 'Fatty' Arbuckle attends a party at which a young actress dies in suspicious circumstances; although acquitted of any involvement his career never recovers.

Tuesday 6: The Peace Arch, commemorating the 1814 Treaty of Ghent which ended the state of war

Left: **Roscoe 'Fatty' Arbuckle.**

September 1921

Margaret Gorman as Miss America 1921.

between the USA and Great Britain, is dedicated on the US/Canada border near Surrey, British Columbia.

Wednesday 7: The first Miss America beauty pageant is held in Atlantic City, New Jersey. Margaret Gorman, 16, is crowned the first Miss America.

Thursday 8: The comedian and singer Sir Harry Secombe is born in Swansea, Wales (died 2001).

Friday 9: Large crowds greet comedian Charlie Chaplin on his return to his native London from Hollywood.

Saturday 10: Three workmen are killed near Liverpool, England, in an explosion while dismantling the captured German submarine *Deutschland.*

Sunday 11: 150 people are killed and US$8m worth of damage caused as tornadoes and flooding hit Texas.

Monday 12: The German Mark falls to its lowest rate to date, equal to one US cent compared to 24 cents in 1914.

Tuesday 13: The White Castle hamburger restaurant, generally regarded as the first fast-food chain in the USA, opens in Wichita, Kansas.

Sir Ernest Shackleton.

Wednesday 14: Sixteen men are killed in an explosion at an oil refinery at Point Breeze, Philadelphia.

Thursday 15: The silent drama film *Little Lord Fauntleroy,* starring Mary Pickford, is released.

Friday 16: 'Felt hat day' takes place in the USA as men make the annual change-over from summer straw 'boaters' to felt hats.

Saturday 17: The British explorer Sir Ernest Shackleton sets sail on his final expedition to Antarctica.

Sunday 18: Paul Ambruster and Louis Ansermier of Switzerland win the Gordon Bennett Cup for the furthest distance travelled in a hot air balloon (476 miles/766km).

Monday 19: The first regular scheduled airline service in Latin America begins, between Barranquilla and Girandot in Colombia.

Charlie Chaplin *(centre)* hosts a party for underprivileged children at the Ritz Hotel during his tour of London.

September 1921

The famous aviator Bernard de Romanet is killed in a plane crash on 23 September.

Tuesday 20: The first radio newsroom in broadcasting history opens at KDKA in Pittsburgh, Pennsylvania.

Wednesday 21: At least 500 people are killed in an explosion at the BASF chemical factory in Oppau, Germany.

Thursday 22: 14 people are killed when the Norwegian cargo ship *Salina* collides with the *Jan Breydel* in the English Channel.

Friday 23: One of France's most celebrated aviators, the Marquis Bernard de Romanet, is killed in a crash while test flying the new Lumiere-de Monge racing plane.

Saturday 24: The US government announces that all occupying troops will be withdrawn from Germany once the US-German peace treaty goes into effect in November.

Sunday 25: Radio broadcasting begins in Bulgaria.

Monday 26: The Riot Act (order to disperse) is read in Belfast for the first time in the city's history, during serious sectarian disturbances.

Tuesday 27: The classical composer Englebert Humperdinck dies aged 67.

Deborah Kerr is born on 30 September.

Wednesday 28: The US pilot Lt John A Macready sets a new altitude record of 35,408ft (10,518m) in a Packard-Le Père LUSAC 11 fighter plane.

Thursday 29: Comedy film star Fatty Arbuckle is released from jail as charges against him for involvement in the death of a young actress on 5 September are dropped.

Friday 30: The actress Deborah Kerr (*The King and I*) is born in Glasgow, Scotland (died 2007).

The crater made by the explosion at the BASF factory in Oppau, Germany, on 21 September. Damage was caused to buildings up to 19 miles away.

October 1921

Saturday 1: French pilot Georges Kirsch wins the *Coupe Deutsch* air race in France, setting an air speed record of 175.6 mph (282.7 km/h).

Sunday 2: The Reverend Robert Runcie MC, Archbishop of Canterbury (1980-1991) is born in Birkenhead (died 2000).

William II, the last king of the German kingdom of Württemberg (abolished 1918) dies aged 73.

Monday 3: Violence erupts in the Malabar region of India as Muslims and Hindus clash after the British authorities lose control.

The Cadle Tabernacle, in Indianapolis, Indiana, opens on 9 October. It is the largest church in the USA to this date.

Tuesday 4: The amateur stunt flyer Madeline Davis is killed in New Jersey while attempting to become the first woman to climb from a moving car to an aeroplane via a rope ladder.

Wednesday 5: The first World Series baseball game is broadcast on US radio.

Thursday 6: The Irish armistice ends as violence between nationalists and Crown forces breaks out in several locations.

The game of table football is patented on 14 October.

Friday 7: Federal agents in Los Angeles announce a crackdown on bootleggers pretending to be Jewish rabbis in order to purchase sacramental wine, which is exempt from Prohibition.

Saturday 8: 22 people are killed when the SS *Rowan* sinks off the coast of Scotland.

William II, last king of Württemberg, dies on 2 October.

Sunday 9: The largest church in the USA to this date, the 11,000 seat Cadle Tabernacle, opens in Indianapolis.

Monday 10: The University of Szeged in Hungary opens.

The novelist James Clavell (*Shogun*) is born in Sydney, Australia (died 1994).

Tuesday 11: Peace talks between Irish nationalists and the British government open in London.

October 1921

Wednesday 12: The Munich *Oktoberfest* ends, after drinkers consume a record 1,894,000 quarts of beer in ten days.

Thursday 13: The Treaty of Kars is signed, establishing the borders between Turkey, Armenia, Azerbaijan and Georgia.

The New York Giants defeat the New York Yankees to win the World Series.

Friday 14: British inventor Harold Searles Thornton patents the game of Table Football.

Babe Ruth.

Saturday 15: The first air service starts between Spain and Morocco.

Rudolf Valentino stars in
The Sheik, released on 21 October.

Sunday 16: Baseball star Babe Ruth is fined a year's pay and suspended for six months after taking part in unlicensed matches during a barnstorming tour.

Monday 17: Heavyweight boxing champion Jack Dempsey denies all allegations of being the third party in a divorce case with vaudeville star Bee Palmer.

Tuesday 18: King Ludwig III, the last ruler of the German kingdom of Bavaria which was abolished in 1918, dies aged 76.

HM King Michael I, the last king of Romania, is born on 25 October.

Wednesday 19: The Prime Minister of Portugal, Antonio Granjo, is assassinated during an uprising in Lisbon.

Thursday 20: Eight people are killed and $10m worth of damage is caused when a hurricane hits Tampa, Florida.

Friday 21: The silent drama film *The Sheik*, starring Rudolph Valentino, premieres in Los Angeles.

Saturday 22: Ireland and England draw 1-1 in the British Home Championship football tournament at Windsor Park, Belfast.

Sunday 23: John Boyd Dunlop, inventor of the pneumatic tyre, dies aged 81.

Monday 24: Spanish colonial troops defeat the Berber rebellion in Morocco.

Tuesday 25: HM King Michael I, the last king of Romania, is born in Sinaia, Romania (died 2017).

Wednesday 26: The Chicago Theatre cinema complex opens in Chicago, Illinois.

HRH Prince Edward, Prince of Wales, departs for a Royal Tour of India and the far east.

HRH Edward, Prince of Wales. *(Portrait by Reginald Grenville Eves)*.

October 1921

Thursday 27: Anti-royalist demonstrations take place in Athens, Greece, against the country's ruler, King Constantine.

Friday 28: Baseball star Babe Ruth begins a nationwide vaudeville (music hall) tour.

Saturday 29: 10 people are killed as severe flooding hits British Columbia, Canada.

Sunday 30: The US Congress announces that 11 November will be marked as a national day of commemoration for the fallen of the Great War.

Monday 31: The Allied war council demands that King Charles IV of Hungary must officially abdicate as part of the post-war settlement.

November 1921

Tuesday 1: A bomb attack by communists takes place on the US Embassy in Lisbon, Portugal.

Wednesday 2: US police announce the break-up of a crime ring which stole Hollywood feature films worth in total $1m, for illegal export to the far eastern market.

Bert Acosta.

Thursday 3: Test pilot Bert Acosta of the USA wins the Pulitzer Trophy for a record breaking speed of 176.7 mph (284.36 km/h) in a Curtis CR-2.

The actor Charles Bronson is born in Ehrenfield, Pennsylvania (died 2003).

Friday 4: Hara Takashi, the prime minister of Japan, is assassinated.

Saturday 5: Princess Fawzia Fuad of Egypt, later Queen of Iran, is born in Alexandria (died 2013).

Sunday 6: The East Karelian Uprising begins, as separatists in East Karelia demand independence from the Soviets in order to join with Finland.

November 1921

Monday 7: The film drama *The Queen of Sheba* starring Betty Blyth and Fritz Leiber is released in the USA.

Tuesday 8: The body of the Unknown Soldier arrives in Washington, DC, on board the US Navy flagship *Olympia*, for ceremonial burial at Arlington National Cemetery.

Wednesday 9: The National Fascist Party of Italy is formed by Benito Mussolini.

Thursday 10: Jennie Kidd Trout, Canada's first woman doctor, dies aged 80.

Friday 11: The Tomb of the Unknown Soldier at Arlington National Cemetery is dedicated by US President Warren G Harding.

The British Legion holds its first 'Poppy Day' to raise funds.

Saturday 12: The Washington Naval Conference on disarmament opens in Washington, DC, attended by representatives of Britain, France, Italy and Japan.

The body of the Unknown Soldier arrives at Washington Navy Yard for burial at Arlington National Ceremony.

Sunday 13: *Ginger Meggs,* Australia's longest-running cartoon serial, is first published in the *Sydney Sunday Sun.*

Monday 14: A bomb placed by an anti-Catholic secularist explodes in front of the statue of the Virgin of Guadalupe in Oaxaca, Mexico. The statue, already believed to have miraculous powers, is unharmed, although the surrounding area is damaged.

Fritz Leiber and Betty Blyth in *The Queen of Sheba.*

Tuesday 15: Isabel, the exiled Princess Imperial of Brazil, who emancipated the country's slaves in 1888, dies aged 75.

Wednesday 16: Gosbank, the state monopoly bank of the Soviet Union, goes into operation.

Thursday 17: HRH Prince Edward, Prince of Wales, arrives in Bombay for the Royal Tour of India.

The first radio broadcast is made in New Zealand.

Friday 18: The British government announces it is cancelling an order for four warships as part of an arms reduction drive.

Saturday 19: The US pilot Bert Acosta sets a world speed record of 197.8mph (318.32 km/h) in a Curtiss CR-2.

Sunday 20: The Catholic Party is victorious in Belgium's General Election.

November 1921

HRH the Prince of Wales greets the crowd at the Calcutta Races. on his 1921-22 tour of India.

Monday 21: Canada is granted its own coat of arms by HM King George V.

Tuesday 22: The Anglo-Afghan Treaty is signed, agreeing that British rule will not extend beyond the Khyber Pass.

The religious leader Abdu'l-Bahá dies on 28 November.

Wednesday 23: The Sheppard-Towner Act introduces US federal funding for maternity and childcare.

Thursday 24: The large asteroid 968-Petunia, in orbit between Jupiter and Mars, is discovered by German astronomer Karl Reinmuth.

Friday 25: Crown Prince Hirohito of Japan is made Regent, ruling in place of his sick father, Emperor Taisho.

Saturday 26: The city of Augusta, Georgia, is devastated by a major fire causing $2.5m worth of damage.

Sunday 27: French military leader Marshal Foch smokes a Peace Pipe with Sioux Indian leader Chief Red Tohahauk in Bismarck, North Dakota, in a thanksgiving ceremony for those Sioux who served with the US Army to liberate France in the Great War.

Monday 28: Abdu'l-Bahá, leader of the Bahá'í religion, dies aged 77.

Tuesday 29: A crowd of 10,000 people attends the funeral of Abdu'l-Bahá, leader of the Bahá'í faith, in Haifa, British Mandatory Palestine (now Israel).

Wednesday 30: The legendary British detective, writer and 'spycatcher' Sir Basil Thomson retires after forty years as head of Special Branch.

Crown Prince Hirohito with his wife, Princess Nagako.

December 1921

Thursday 1: *The Lucky Dog*, the first film in which comedians Stan Laurel and Oliver Hardy both appear, is released.

Friday 2: Rioting and looting breaks out in Vienna, Austria, following severe food shortages.

Saturday 3: The Egyptian Football Association is founded.

Sunday 4: The singer Deanna Durbin is born in Winnipeg, Canada (died 2013).

Monday 5: West Australian Airways, the first regular scheduled airline service in Australia, begins operation.

Tuesday 6: The Anglo-Irish Treaty is signed, establishing the semi-autonomous Irish Free State and ending the Irish War of Independence.

Laurel and Hardy *(above)* make their first film together on 1 December.

Agnes Macphail becomes the first woman MP in Canada.

The 1921 Nobel Prize winners are announced on 10 December.

They include Anatole France *(left)* and Albert Enstein *(right).*

Wednesday 7: Sir Edward Carson, Ulster Unionist leader, announces that the Anglo-Irish Treaty is 'abject humiliation' for Great Britain.

Thursday 8: 18 people are killed when severe storms hit Newfoundland.

On 9 December J W Gott becomes the last person to be jailed in England for blasphemy.

Friday 9: John William Gott becomes the last person in England to be imprisoned for blasphemy after publishing a series of attacks on Christianity.

Saturday 10: The 1921 Nobel Prize winners are announced, including Albert Einstein for Physics and Anatole France for Literature.

Sunday 11: The actress Liz Smith, best known for her role as Nana in the BBC sitcom *The Royle Family* and Letitia Cropley in *The Vicar of Dibley,* is born in Scunthorpe, Lincolnshire (died 2016).

December 1921

Alvis cars are first produced on 14 December.
Above: an early Alvis sports model.

Monday 12: British proposals to ban the use of submarines in warfare are rejected at the Washington arms reduction talks.

Tuesday 13: The Four Power Treaty is signed by the USA, UK, France and Japan defining colonial possessions in the Pacific.

Wednesday 14: The Alvis car marque is introduced in England by TG John and Company of Coventry.

Thursday 15: Alan Freed, the US disc jockey who popularised the term 'rock and roll', is born in Windber, PA (died 1965).

The proposed union of all Presbyterian and Reformed church denominations in the USA is deferred indefinitely, due to disagreements.

The composer Saint-Saëns dies on 16 December.

Friday 16: The composer Camille Saint-Saëns (*Carnival of the Animals*) dies aged 86.

Saturday 17: The Hollywood star Constance Talmadge announces her divorce from husband John Pialoglou on

December 1921

The British Prime Minister David Lloyd George (left) meets with the Prime Minister of France, Aristide Briand, for talks on 20 December.

the grounds of his disapproval of her acting career.

The US Congress authorises the payment of $20m for famine relief in Soviet Russia.

Sunday 18: The Polish national football team plays its first game as an independent country, losing 1-0 to Hungary in Budapest.

Monday 19: The Roman Catholic Archbishop of New York, PJ Hayes, denounces divorce and birth control as 'pagan' in his Christmas sermon.

Tuesday 20: The British Prime Minister David Lloyd-George and his French counterpart, Aristide Briand, meet in London to discuss German war reparations.

Wednesday 21: The Anglo-American financier Sir Edgar Speyer, who helped finance the building of the London Underground, is stripped of his British citizenship after allegations of spying for Germany in the First World War.

The *Potez IX*.

Thursday 22: France's *Potez IX* passenger

December 1921

aeroplane is launched at the Paris Air Show.

Sobhuza II is proclaimed King of Swaziland; he goes on to have the longest reign (82 years) of any sovereign in history.

Friday 23: The Workers' Party of America is founded. The word 'communist' is not included in its title for fear of legal action.

Saturday 24: The comedian Jimmy Clitheroe (*The Clitheroe Kid*) is born in Lancashire, England (died 1973).

1,000 illegal immigrants are released from detention on New York City's Ellis Island on condition that they return within 90 days for deportation.

Sunday 25: 44 people are killed and $1m worth of damage is caused as tornadoes hit the south-eastern USA.

Monday 26: Martial law is imposed by the British authorities in Port Said, Egypt, following nationalist disturbances.

Tuesday 27: HRH the Prince of Wales is guest of honour at the Viceroy's Cup race meeting in Calcutta, as part of his Indian tour.

Wednesday 28: US motion picture makers demand import tariffs for foreign films, claiming they take work away from American studios.

Thursday 29: William Lyon Mackenzie King becomes Prime Minister of Canada.

Friday 30: Sergei Prokofiev's satirical opera, *The Love for Three Oranges* is first performed, at the Auditorium Theatre in Chicago, Illinois.

Saturday 31: Tennis player Rice Gemmel wins the 1921 Australasian Championships in Perth, Australia.

Printed in Great Britain
by Amazon

68167608R00037